# POCKETKNIFE
# MAKING
## for Beginners

## Stefan Steigerwald and Peter Fronteddu

4880 Lower Valley Road Atglen, Pennsylvania 19310

**Other Schiffer Books By The Author:**
*The Lockback Folding Knife: From Design to Completion*, 978-0-7643-3509-9, $29.99

**Other Schiffer Books on Related Subjects:**
*Basic Knife Making: From Raw Steel to a Finished Stub Tang Knife*, 978-0-7643-3508-2, $29.99

First published as *Klappmesser bauen für Anfänger* by Wieland Verlag GmbH.

Translated from German by Ingrid Elser and John Guess.

Library of Congress Control Number: 2011931316

Designed by "Sue"
Type set in Gill Sans Std/Minion Pro

ISBN: 978-0-7643-3847-2
Printed in China

Schiffer Books are available at special discounts for bulk purchases for sales promotions or premiums. Special editions, including personalized covers, corporate imprints, and excerpts can be created in large quantities for special needs. For more information contact the publisher:

Published by Schiffer Publishing Ltd.
4880 Lower Valley Road
Atglen, PA 19310
Phone: (610) 593-1777;
Fax: (610) 593-2002
E-mail: Info@schifferbooks.com

For the largest selection of fine reference books on this and related subjects,
please visit our website at:
**www.schifferbooks.com**
We are always looking for people to write books on new and related subjects.
If you have an idea for a book, please contact us at
proposals@schifferbooks.com

This book may be purchased from the publisher. Include $5.00 for shipping. Please try your bookstore first. You may write for a free catalog.

In Europe, Schiffer books are distributed by
Bushwood Books
6 Marksbury Ave.
Kew Gardens
Surrey TW9 4JF England
Phone: 44 (0) 20 8392 8585;
Fax: 44 (0) 20 8392 9876
E-mail: info@bushwoodbooks.co.uk
Website: www.bushwoodbooks.co.uk

# CONTENTS

# A Few Words Up Front

Knifemaking as a hobby is becoming increasingly popular. More and more people are discovering how much joy it can be to create such a pretty, and also practical, device on their own. Constructing a folding knife is especially attractive but also poses special difficulties of its own. Basically, a knife with a moveable blade is a far greater challenge with respect to construction and craftsmanship than a fixed blade.

Nevertheless, there are also simple solutions at hand: not using a locking mechanism makes work easier. In addition to that, folding knives without locks are now en vogue again. Thus classic folders, which are opened using both hands, are back in the center of interest, as are folding knives without any locking mechanism. This book is about the latter type of knife. They are the simplest kind of folders and thus comprise an ideal beginning for knifemakers new to folding knives.

By means of this workshop series, we want to help you with all types of technical questions and avoid pitfalls. This series of books assembles a multitude of themes all around knifemaking in a way that enables you to follow and execute each step by yourself.

The focus is to provide a book that is easy to use in the workshop. Thus all the volumes have a wire binding. This way, the book stays open when you put it down on your workbench. Also, we made the size of the images and fonts big enough so the book is easy to read as you're working.

We have tried to explain every step in the most comprehensive way. But before you pick up your tools, you should read the descriptions and explanations first. You'll know what to expect and won't be confronted with unpleasant surprises later on.

My heartfelt thanks goes to Stefan Steigerwald, who often and enthusiastically comes up with new themes and also explores new methods with respect to practical work. Peter Fronteddu once again documented every step of work in detail with his camera and throughout the text of this volume. Together they make a really great team.

As you use this book I hope your work is fun and successful!

Hans Joachim Wieland
Chief Editor, *MESSER MAGAZIN* (*Knife Magazine*)

Constructing a folding knife using only a few machines and tools was a new technical frontier for me. Prior to all the efforts that go into the finishing process, I'm otherwise used to using all the great machines that are surrounding me in my workshop. Giving up these habits and using simple tools instead wasn't always easy for me.

But this is exactly what keeps us going: new challenges, shapes, and materials. If you are using this book to tackle folding knives, you'll see how complex the whole issue is. But don't be afraid: it will all turn out well—in a very pivotal sense.

Even Peter sometimes was keen on trading his camera for a file. I hope that I don't lose him to the knifemaker's world because of our book projects. He ought to stay with us as a photographer and author.

Stefan Steigerwald

After describing quite complicated knife projects in the last few volumes, this time we wanted to come up with something simpler with respect to construction, and simpler and quicker in manufacturing—utility knives that can be built without a big collection of power tools and machines.

Although a slipjoint folding knife looks quite simple at first glance, as you start understanding the design, you realize that it's not that easy at all because here—similar to a backlock—the backspring fulfills several functions at once.

As usual, we have documented every step of the process and rather than omit anything, we even added descriptions of intermediate steps. Whoever follows the manual step by step and uses a template before starting to build at random will soon hold a functioning slipjoint folding knife in their hands.

But my favorite among these knives was only found towards the end of the production: it's the friction folder. Out of a blade, a strip of metal, a piece of wood, and a few rivets, a usable pocket knife was constructed quite rapidly.

Among pocket knife enthusiasts, I belong to the "mechanics faction." The more complicated the locking mechanism, the more interesting a knife is to me. Usually. The friction folder is the exception. A knife that has just the necessary parts has a special charm that you can hardly escape.

Such a knife is also rather quick to build. The material doesn't have to be expensive and with the exception of a drill press machine and a few files and sandpaper, no tools are used beyond common shop tools. In addition to this, a friction folder is very lightweight—the ideal knife for a little snack between work. Rye bread, ham, and the homemade folder. Have fun and bon appetit!

Peter Fronteddu

# Preparation

## 1.1 In General

With respect to building a slipjoint, as well as a friction folder, there are different approaches. We settled on using as many simple tools as possible—not the big industrial machine shop toys that Stefan Steigerwald is used to. But this approach may not be for every interested knifemaker. Slipjoint and friction folders are unspoilt, simple constructions. Many traditional pocket knives have been manufactured in this style for decades, maybe even centuries—like the Laguiole in France or the Resolza from Sardinia. And as simple and very reasonable utility knives, they still prove to be successful nowadays, despite new technological developments.

Compared to linerlocks or backlocks, these knife types require fewer parts for construction. The friction folder, in particular, doesn't demand the tight tolerances that have to be kept with complicated locking mechanisms. The knives were riveted at the handle and the pivot, they were not—as Stefan Steigerwald usually does—screwed together. The tight fit is accomplished by means of vigorously hitting the rivets. Some parts, the clamp or blade pivot, for example, were made from whatever happened to be laying around the workshop or the house.

Of course, slipjoints or friction folders can also be constructed by means of different technical solutions and processes. As in our previous knifemaking guides, we describe Stefan Steigerwald's methods. Some are the same as those he uses for folders in general, but variations occurred when dealing with specific pieces of work. Thus this volume is not meant to be a strict manual for building a folder. It is rather meant to stimulate and encourage the reader to try building a folding knife of his/her own. You'll find your own way of doing it through your work.

Of course, there had to be the typical Steigerwald scale knife once again, and for one slipjoint model, Damascus steel with just the right dimensions was laying on the workbench. But there are easier ways, as pointed out by the examples.

Finally, a remark with respect to work safety: in order to take good photos of each individual work step, we refrained from the usual precautions with respect to safety. Everybody who is about to start building a knife should look up the guidelines necessary for safety at work. Among these are wearing protective goggles and securely clamping or otherwise fixing the parts you are working with. This is especially the case for working with power tools.

## 1.2 Choice of Materials

Traditional materials have been used to build classic slipjoints and friction folders for a long time. The blades are mostly made of simple carbon steels, but nowadays stainless steels like 440A, 440B, Sandvik 12C27, or similar steels are increasingly used. For the handles, mainly natural materials, like suitable kinds of wood, horn, or bones were used. Of course, there is nothing that says you can't use modern and expensive materials when taking on simple knife construction. A slipjoint with powder metallurgical steel, titanium liners, and handle scales made of carbon fiber has its special appeal. For the beginners, however, for whom this volume is focused, several factors contribute to the choice of materials:

1. Availability: Parts like the pivot of a friction folder, the clamp, or the handle of plain wood can be found in a corner of your workshop. Building something from available parts can be very exciting and also saves money.

2. Workability: Basically, every knife can be built by means of a file, a drill, and a bit of sandpaper. But it is easier to use a blade steel that can be filed and polished easily. Liners made out of nickel silver or brass are also easier to work with compared to steel or titanium.

3. Price: For somebody who has just started to work on their very first knife, it doesn't make sense to do so with the most expensive materials. Apart from workability, botching a blade of Crucible Particle Metallurgy (CPM) or Damascus, liners of titanium, and handle scales of mother-of-pearl is an annoying waste of money. Time is never wasted, it is a period of learning. And during this period, rather plain materials, which are

nevertheless of appropriate quality, help to get the job done. It is more reasonable to use plain materials passionately than to work with a heap of expensive raw parts only half-heartedly.

## 1.2.1 Blade Steel

A treatise on the pros and cons of all the steels available on the market would go far beyond the scope of this book.

In essence, the steels used for building knives can be divided into three categories: carbon steels/low-alloy steels, high-alloy/stainless steels, and powder metallurgical steels, which are being used more and more.

Carbon steels or low-alloy steels are mainly or almost exclusively made of iron and carbon. Typical examples are 1095, CK60, CK75, or 1.2842. The typical "disadvantage" of these types of steel is the fact that they are not stainless (none of the steels that can be hardened are truly stainless). If you don't require stainless steel for the knife you are making, these kinds of steel are not a bad choice at all. They are cheap, can be heat treated quite easily by the knifemaker, are malleable, and easy to work with and sharpen. They can be hardened to quite high values while the whole blade, and the microscopic parts of the edge, still stay sufficiently stable.

Carbon steels usually form relatively small carbides— carbon compounds that act like extremely hard and abrasive-resistant microscopic "grains" within the "matrix," or structure, of the steel. These small carbides enable a very fine and very stable structure. Thus carbon steels are a first choice for those who are making a knife that not only cuts well but keeps its edge well. This trend for carbon steels can also be seen when looking at the increasing number of knives available with "rusting" blades.

Most knives on the market come with blades made of high-alloy stainless steel. Typical examples of this category are the steel types

ATS-34, 440C, 154-CM, AUS-8, 12C27, and 1.4034. With a chromium content of 13% inside the matrix of the finished blade, these steels are practically "stainless." Besides chromium, these alloys contain other elements such as vanadium or molybdenum. These partially form rather big carbides, which act almost like the teeth of a saw inside the blade edge. This feature, to a certain extent, is favored because it enhances the effectiveness of drawing cuts.

A blade of such stainless steel holds the edge quite well, but is not as fine and compact as a blade made of carbon steel. Blades of stainless steel are, hardened to the same value, also less stable than those of carbon steel—but this doesn't matter with respect to the dimensions of the blade of our pocket knife. In general, the optimal hardness tends to be lower than the hardness of pure carbon steel.

One step further there are the very high-alloy stainless steels, which are produced by means of a powder-metallurgical process. Among these so-called PM-steels are CPM-S30V, S60V, S90V, RWL-34, Vanadis, ZDP-189, and CPM-154. This kind of manufacturing leads to very small, evenly spread carbides and a fine matrix. Blades of powder-metallurgically produced steel are thus more flexible but can also have very fine edges.

Another area comprises Damascus steels. Because of the upswing of bladesmithing—be it hobby or profession— during recent years, a great variety of manually forged Damascus is now available. Most of this Damascus is made from carbon steel, little is stainless Damascus. In addition, there exists a great variety of powder-metallurgically produced, stainless Damascus made by the Swedish company Damasteel.

Nowadays, using Damascus is more a question of aesthetics. With respect to the available quality of mono steels, fusing different types of steels hardly increases the quality. Even for manually forged Damascus optimized for great performance, a possible increase in quality is not proportionate to effort and price. But this doesn't mean that Damascus shouldn't be used in principle—after all, a certain amount of individuality can't be balanced with money.

The discussion about which kinds of steel are "best" for knives is often quite heated. The true answer is: there is no best steel. Depending on the planned use for the knife, your own skills, and the price, you'll have to decide on a compromise. Besides, in the discussion about choosing steel, questions about the appropriate heat treatment and the best edge shape for the planned purpose are quite often neglected. Both parameters have at least the same effect on the cutting ability and the general effectiveness as the choice of material.

Only by means of the proper heat treatment, optimized with respect to material and use, can the steel achieve the desired quality (hardness, flexibility, resistance against rusting, smoothness of the edge). Heat treatment that isn't optimized means gambling away the potential of the steel. Thus it is recommended to use a type of steel for which the process of heat treatment is well-known and under control—regardless of whether you harden the steel yourself or send it away for hardening.

The blade shape has a decisive influence on cutting ability and the stability of a blade. The edge angle determines how much force you need for cutting. The smaller the angle, the sharper the edge and thus the less pressure you have to apply while cutting. On the other hand, the edge has to be tuned to steel and application. A blade with a hollow grind and very thin edge would get stuck in the material it was cutting and the edge would soon be ruined. A blade with spherical grind, better suited for this purpose, is less suited for pressing cuts. A flat grind is more robust and easier to manufacture, a perfectly made hollow grind requires more experience (and more machines) with grinding. But by means of the special geometry of the hollow grind, you can achieve a fine edge even with relatively thick blades. Apart from this, the hollow grind looks really noble.

The heat treatment of all blades created within the framework of this book was contracted to a company experienced in heat treating the steels used. This also saves a lot of time for the knifemaker. Since the blades are hardened within a vacuum furnace, almost no cinder (layer of oxides) is created in the process, which would have to be ground off afterwards. Also, it is possible to grind and polish the blade almost to completion prior to hardening. So it is sufficient to leave just two tenths of a millimeter of material at the edge prior to heat treatment.

In deciding upon blade material for our slipjoints and friction folders, besides the theory of steels, practical questions are also of importance—the steel should be cheap and easy to work on with simple means. Since "stainless" is always a matter of taste, we decided upon the stainless steel N690 made by Boehler, an Austrian manufacturer. This steel provides a good compromise between price and capabilities, it is easy to work with and polish, and the heat treatment company is up to the task of hardening it.

N690 can also be annealed to the hardness of a spring without any problems, which is advantageous because the same material can be used for the blade and the backspring. This means you don't have to grind another piece of steel to the same thickness as the blade.

Damascus steel was used for the blade and liners of the upscale version of our slipjoint folder.

# 1.2.2 Materials for Handles and Other Parts

For the other parts, we also chose materials that were easy to acquire, easy to work with, and not too expensive. For the liners we used brass and nickel silver, and for the bolsters we used bronze. The rivets can be made of stainless steel or bronze. For the screwed pivot, we used a toggle bolt purchased at a home improvement store.

For the handles we used whatever was lying around in the workshop at that time: kudu horn, ziricote wood, and bog oak (admittedly, in Stefan Steigerwald's workshop lots of things are laying around). All kinds of woods can be used, as long as they are hard and dry enough not to warp. You have to be especially careful with respect to this. Since we want to

rivet our knives and not screw them together, warped or even ruptured handle scales can't be replaced easily. To be on the safe side, use artificial materials such as G-10, micarta, carbon fiber, or stabilized wood.

Please be aware that many materials used for making knives pose a health risk while working with them. The dust of many tropical woods is toxic and can cause allergic reactions, as can the dust and fibers of compounds. Stabilized woods sometimes contain epoxy resins, mother-of-pearl contains arsenic, and carbon fibers accumulate in your lungs. Be sure to use suitable breathing masks and exhaust fans when working.

Finally, when choosing the appropriate materials for your knife, vendors specializing in knifemaking supplies are usually very helpful.

## 1.3 Tools

## 1.3.1 The File: The Most Important Tool

Files differ in size, body shape, cut, and the shape of their teeth. Rasps, in contrast to files, have separately cut teeth. If these teeth are cut (negative rake angle) they act as scrapers. Milled teeth (positive rake angle) cut.

Besides the profile of the teeth, files differ in the number and order of the teeth on the file body.

The term "file cut" describes the complete number of teeth on the file which were created on the file body by stroking, cutting, or milling. In general, the harder the material you're working with, the smoother the file cut should be.

For softer material, including soft metal, files with cut 1 should be used. The sufficiently wide distance between the teeth assures that no material gets stuck and clumps up on the file. For hard materials, files with cut 2 are used. On those, the so-called down-cut has an angle of about 50°, the up-cut crosses at an angle of about 70°. The up-cut creates the actual edge, the crossing down-cut (most times cut deeper into the file body than the up-cut) ought to break off the shavings. Because of the angle, the teeth are set alternately. So score marks on the material are avoided.

## GRADES OF FILE CUTS

Depending on their length, files of the same cut have different cut numbers. Swiss-pattern files are available in seven cuts and get progressively finer as the cut number goes up. American-pattern files are available in three cuts. The number of cuts per centimeter for Swiss-pattern files and the corresponding American-pattern equivalents is as follows:

| Swiss-pattern Cut No. | American-pattern Equivalent | Cuts per centimeter |
| --- | --- | --- |
| 00 | | ? |
| 0 | | 4.5 – 10 |
| 1 | Bastard | 5.3 – 16 |
| 2 | Second Cut | 10 – 25 |
| 3 | Smooth Cut | 14 – 35 |
| 4 | | 25 – 50 |
| 6 | | 40 – 71 |

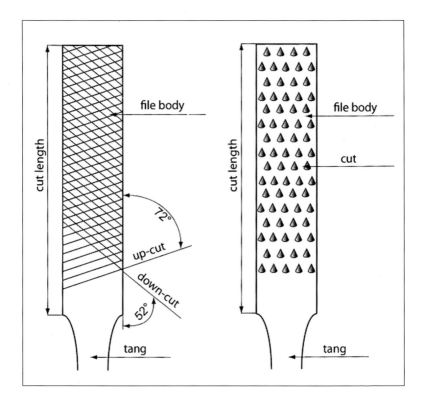

The cut number designates the number of cuts per centimeter. The grade of cut is a means to distinguish between the various files. Common Swiss-pattern files bear the grades 00 or 0 (coarse files for wood and soft materials), cut number 1 (medium cut files), and cut numbers 2, 3, 4, and 6 (smooth cut files).

Files are available in a wide variety of shapes: rectangular, triangular, round, diamond-shaped, or semicircular. For flat surfaces, usually flat or semicircular files are used. With a mill saw file, which has a single-cut at the rounded edge, we work towards the shoulder (the short, blunt part of the blade past the edge). We do this to achieve a rounded transition while working on a flat surface.

There are other ways: the transition at the shoulder can be filed with a round file as well. For the rest of the surface then a file should be used that has no cut at the sides so no rough edge will be created around the shoulder.

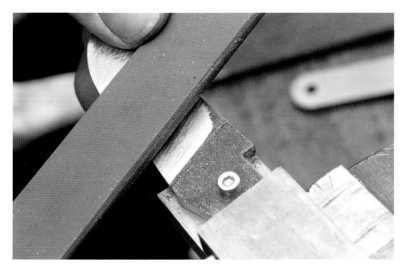

Anything but a simple tool—a wide range of files is available.

Files should be cleaned on a regular base with a file card. When shavings are stuck between the teeth, the file is blunt.

## 1.3.2 Sandpaper/Abrasive Cloth

As with tools in general, it pays not to be stingy with respect to the quality of sandpaper or abrasive cloth. A tip: sandpaper should be kept separated according to grit in folders. This way you won't have any loose, coarse grains on your finer sandpaper.

For sanding a plane surface we need a hard substrate (wood, metal). This is especially important for working at transition points, including the shoulder. This will get you clear, well-defined corners. For sanding rounded areas, around the handle, for example, we use abrasive cloth or abrasive fleece.

It is important that you complete each step of your sanding work. Before changing to the next finer grit, the polish has to be regular and without a hitch. Also, with each new grit number we start sanding at a 90° angle from the previous direction of sanding.

## 1.3.3 Working with Alignment Pins and Drilling Holes

While working on the parts of the knife that need accurate positioning (spring, pivot, etc.), we fix their position with prepared drill holes and alignment pins. As an alternative, rolled material can also be used, e.g. rods of stainless steel, brass, or similar materials. Later on the knife will be riveted using the same drill holes.

In order to achieve straight drill holes, we glue the liners together and drill the holes for the pivot and the handle rivets in a single step of work. Of course, the liners also have to be aligned perpendicular to the drill in order to be aligned perfectly with respect to each other and for the blade to be centered correctly within the frame.

In general, we drill the holes undersized and afterwards ream them up to the right size. For a blade pivot of 3.0 mm (0.118"), we first drill to 2.8 mm (0.110") and then ream to 3.0 mm. This way the pivot doesn't have any play inside the drill hole. Working with used reamers, which have a diameter that is just below a normal reamer, is no disadvantage. In fact, it results in a tighter fit. And when using riveted joints for the pivot or handle, you have a bit more play.

## 1.3.4 Washers

For assembling the knife we also need proper washers, usually of teflon or bronze. Teflon washers are easy to construct. With punch pliers and scissors, or with various hollow punches, the washers are cut to size or punched out of the material. As a raw material, either pure teflon or teflon strengthened with woven fabric are available in a wide variety of thicknesses.

Teflon washers stamped neatly into discs with a center punch.

Teflon washers can pick up small dust particles. But, especially for smaller diameters, teflon is not able to resist lots of pressure; the lateral stability of the blade bearing thus is not very high.

Bronze washers take a lot of effort to fabricate. We have to punch holes into the sheet of bronze, then roughly cut out the pieces, put them onto a mandrel and shape to size on the lathe. For punching the center holes of the bronze washers we used a tool designed specifically for this task.

Manufactured bronze washers are only available in a few sizes. They are less resistant to dirt because they are not as soft as teflon. Small particles of dirt are thus pressed onto the blade.

The advantage of using bronze is that there is higher stability, compared to teflon. Therefore the blade can be adjusted to a higher degree, the movements also stay the same over a long period of time, and they are also more exact. In addition, bronze washers are also self-lubricating. Sheet metal for bronze washers is available as raw material in various thicknesses (e.g. as bearing bronze, tin bronze, etc).

The thickness of the washers depends on how tight the fit of the blade should be. Usually the thickness is 0.1 mm (0.003") or 0.2 mm (0.007"). For a bit more space between parts, a thickness of 0.3 mm (0.011") or up to a maximum of 0.5 mm (0.019") can be used.

Washers can also be omitted altogether. In this case, the blade moves along the liners directly. This requires outstanding surface quality. And besides that, the surface of the liners should be at least 5 to 10 Rockwell grades (HRC) below that of the blade. Liners of platinum, steel, or non-ferrous metals are appropriate for the job. The disadvantage of making

Bronze washers are punched from a strip with a special tool.

Several raw washers are roughly cut out, then chucked on the lathe and turned.

a knife without a washer, besides the complicated surface treatment, are that this type of construction is also sensitive to very small dust particles and the unevenness of the material.

## 1.3.5 Vise

A vise lasts for an entire lifetime—usually. Take care that the guidance elements are more or less without play and the jaws—when closed—are level. During our work we use them as a back stop to achieve a clean edge when filing. The vise shouldn't be too lightweight either. The heavier the vise, the better it dampens the vibrations created while filing or polishing.

## 1.3.6 Drill Press

In order to drill some holes, a simple drill press from a home improvement store is sufficient. You have to take care that the table is perpendicular to the drill spindle. The adjustable elements of a press, a swivel table or swivel head, are mostly unnecessary and do not enhance precision.

With respect to machines and power tools for the workshop, it is a great idea to search for used, high-quality brand-name models. These are much better to work with than cheap tools of unknown origin.

# Slipjoint Folding Knife

With slipjoint folders, the open and closed blade is held in place by a spring under pressure. So slipjoints don't have a locking mechanism like backlock folders, which are otherwise similar in construction and which have a hammer-like spring keeping the blade in open position. In addition to holding the blade, the backspring is also the end stop for the open blade.

There are several ways to construct the end stop for the blade in closed position. A lot of traditional knives don't have any end stop at all—when closed, the blade hits the backspring. More gentle to the blade is a well-defined end stop that keeps the edge away from the backspring. To achieve this, you can shape the blade and backspring in a way that, when closed, the blade foot hits the corresponding part of the backspring before the edge touches the back of the handle.

Another obvious possibility is to use a stop pin, i.e. a separate pin, for stopping the blade. We chose this variation because this construction method is, in the end, easier to execute. In addition to this, small errors in construction and assembly of the folder are easier to correct. The important issues related to this are depicted in the images on pages 51 through 53.

## 2.1 Designing and Drawing a Template

On graph paper we draw three guide lines: the two vertical lines determine the handle length. In addition, we draw the topmost part of the back, and thus determine the height of the handle and the back of the blade. When this is done, we sketch the outline of the handle.

Towards the blade, the handle receives a small guard. It prevents one's fingers from slipping onto the edge while working with the knife. At the same time, we gain more space for the tang. The tang will be covered by the guard later on, so no parts will stick out when the folding knife is closed.

Determine the handle length by drawing two lines. A third line determines the back of our knife. Draw the contours of the handle within these boundaries.

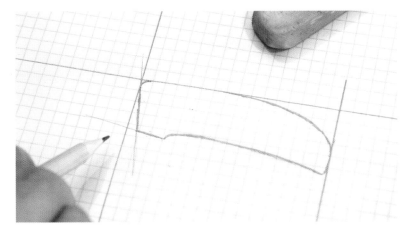

Draw the guard at the front of the handle.

In order to determine the position of the blade pivot, we draw a line parallel to the front end of the handle about 8 mm (0.315") farther back. The closer to the front the pivot is drawn, the longer the blade will be in relation to the handle. But we still need enough space for the tang (locking mechanism, washers).

To have enough room for spacers and an edge inside the handle when the folder is closed, the center point of the pivot should be a bit below the center of that line. If the pivot is positioned even lower, the blade won't be covered far enough when the knife is closed.

Starting from the center of the pivot, we use a compass to determine the maximum length of the blade. With a curve template or freehand, the desired blade contour is drawn within the boundaries marked with the compass.

After drawing the edge we gain a first impression of our knife. We will see whether the draft will work in three dimensions during the next step, making a template.

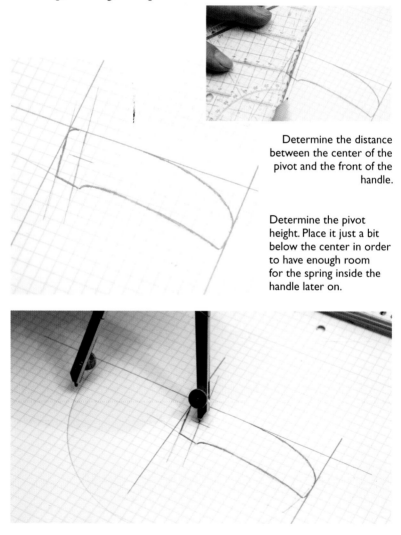

Determine the distance between the center of the pivot and the front of the handle.

Determine the pivot height. Place it just a bit below the center in order to have enough room for the spring inside the handle later on.

Draw the blade's maximum possible length. This is the same length as the distance between the center of the pivot and the end of the handle.

Draw the shape of the blade. A curve template makes it easier to find the right contours.

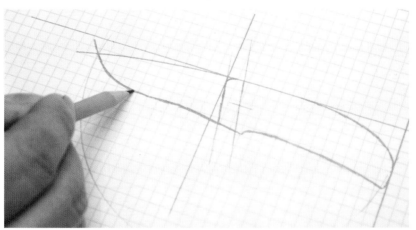

The rough sketch of our knife is finished.

Cut out the blade and handle and create a cardboard template of both. Paste the blade with enough material left over for designing the tang later on. A thumbtack is used as a preliminary blade pivot.

The template allows us to check whether the outlines of the blade and handle fit together. The blade should vanish inside the handle as much as possible. The blade tip has to be covered completely by the handle. Open, as well as closed, no sharp corners should stick out anywhere.

Glue the blade and handle onto cardboard. Cut along the contours, leaving enough material behind the blade to adjust the tang later on.

Copy the sketch and cut out the knife.

Use a thumbtack as the blade pivot for the template.

The handle and blade of the finished template are "mounted."

If necessary, we adjust the blade and back with scissors. The part of the tang that is longer than the handle when closed is cut off.

Inside the handle there has to be enough room for the backspring. We close our "knife" far enough that the tip is covered by the handle. Later the spring will be located between the edge and the back of the handle. More space is not available—so, if necessary, we have to adjust the shape of the blade right now. Once everything fits together,

Close the knife. The tip of the blade must be covered by the handle; if necessary, we refine. The outer contour of the handle determines the maximum size of the tang.

Cut off the protruding end of the tang.

we transfer the outline of the blade onto the inside of the handle template. This way we can start to see the shape the backspring will have later on.

We perform another functional test—is anything poking out, does the blade fit inside the handle, is there enough space for the backspring? It's easier to cut cardboard now than steel later.

Next in line is the construction of the tang. The spring moves along the tang each time the folder is opened or closed. The part on which it is gliding thus has to be rounded. With our compass we draw a circle around the center of the pivot. Since the blade should always move smoothly, the area with which the tang touches liners and washers should be large enough. Thus the radius should be as big as possible within the boundaries of the handle outlines.

Now draw the pocket where the spring will rest. Close to the rounded edge of the handle, we mark the spot where the spring ends. At exactly this spot on the blade, we draw the front edge of the pocket.

The backspring should move freely around the blade tang. For this we first draw a circle around the blade pivot.

We mark the position where the spring reaches.

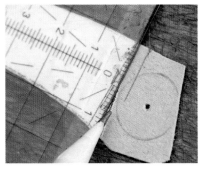

The line depicts the front edge of the pocket for the spring.

Now determine the height of the pocket.

Thereafter the height of the pocket is determined. The distance between the center of the pivot and the rear wall of the pocket is (besides the strength of the spring) the decisive factor with respect to the force keeping the blade in open position. The farther back this spot is positioned (thus a deeper pocket), the better the leverage of the spring. To have enough area for a sufficient bearing (big washers) the working point of the spring (depth of the pocket) should not be too far down.

The next step is to draw the spring. For support we mark the position of the blade edge of the closed folder. The spring is located between this line and the back of the handle. We draw it up to the rear edge of the tang.

The points where we attach the backspring are marked—the knife will be riveted at these spots later on. The head of the spring and the first of the rivets have to be separated by a sufficient distance so there is enough clearance for work. The distance should also not be too small, otherwise the torque will be too high.

Cut out the pocket and mount the blade and handle template. Now draw the spring.

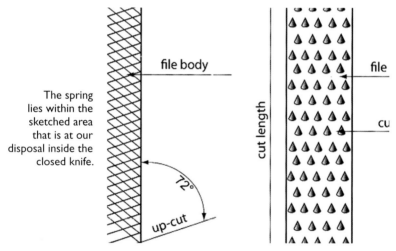

The spring lies within the sketched area that is at our disposal inside the closed knife.

file body

72°

up-cut

cut length

file

cu

The hammer-shaped end of the spring reaches up to the rear end of the tang.

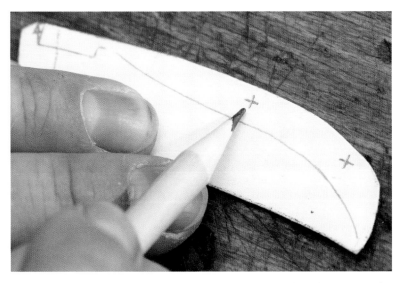

Mark the positions for
mounting the spring.

Important:
there must
be sufficient
space between
the spring and
the blade of
the knife.

The closed blade should hit a stop pin. For this we mark the end stop. The position should be as far to the front as possible to achieve maximum blade length.

When the knife is open, the tang should stop at the front end of the backspring. Prior to transferring the outlines onto the material used for the knife, we should check its function once again with the template.

For our knife we also created a functional template made of brass. This brass template is an even better sample for checking the knife's actions and dimensions. We used alignment pins for the stop pin, pivot, and rivets. If you want to build several models of the same design, brass or aluminum templates are also helpful.

Later the template for the handle is copied onto the material used for the liners—in our case, a sheet of nickel silver with a thickness of 1.0 mm (0.039").

Draw the recess in the blade, which will rest against the stop pin. The pin is positioned as far forward on the knife as possible. Thus the corresponding recess will not be positioned in the blade.

Now mark the position of the stop pin inside the handle. Once again, check the function of the template.

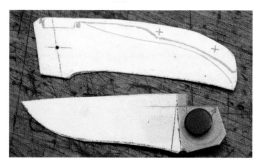

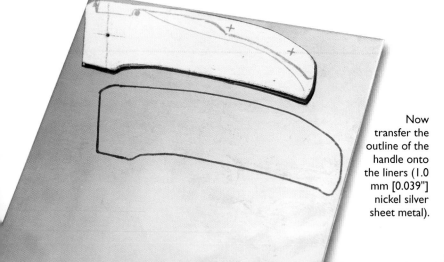

Now transfer the outline of the handle onto the liners (1.0 mm [0.039"] nickel silver sheet metal).

## 2.2 Working on the Handle

Using a waterproof felt pen, we transfer the handle contours onto the material. With a center punch we mark the positions of the blade pivot and rivets for the spring and stop pin.

We use a hacksaw to cut out the coarse shape. Then we use sandpaper for a brief polish to make sure the surfaces are clean and all burrs are removed.

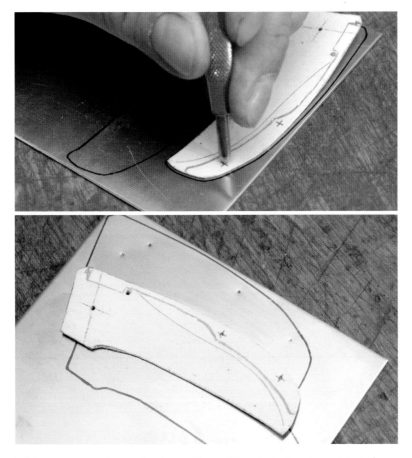

With a center punch, transfer the positions of the pivot, stop pin, and rivets from the cardboard template.

Roughly cut out the liners.

With sand paper (grit P240), remove burrs from the blanks.

With superglue, we then fix both blanks—the marked liner on top. We always drill through both liners at the same time to make completely vertical drill holes.

Glue the liners together with superglue.

Now drill with a 2.8 mm (0.110") bit.

With a reamer, widen the hole to 3.0 mm (0.118").

Now we drill the marked holes. To work accurately, drill the holes with 0.1 mm (0.003") to 0.2 mm (0.007") less in diameter and then use a reamer to widen the holes to their final size. For our knife we need 3.0 mm (0.118") for the pivot and 2.0 mm (0.078") for the spacers and stop pin. While reaming, make sure the rotational speed is slow and the bit is well lubricated.

If necessary, the outlines are once again drawn using the template. The drill holes are used as a marker when the template is positioned.

With a file, we shape the contour. For this we clamp the liners, which are still glued together, into the vise. With aptly shaped blocks, we sand up to a grit of P240. To be absolutely sure the pieces stay together properly, you can use alignment pins in addition to the superglue.

Once the holes are drilled and reamed, draw the outline again.

With a file, shape the contours of the liners (still glued).

After that we refine with sand paper (P240) and a suitable sanding block.

For the bottom we use a rounded sanding block to achieve a clean radius at the guard.

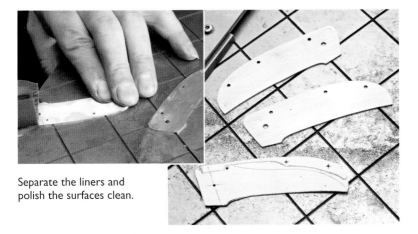

Separate the liners and polish the surfaces clean.

Here are liners smoothly polished up to P600.

Separate both liners from each other—usually they will come apart by knocking them lightly on a hard surface. Clean the liner surfaces with sandpaper to remove any glue residue.

Now polish both liners on all sides up to grit P600. For the area around the guard, we use a rounded sanding block.

## 2.3 Creating the Blade

First of all, we check to make sure the blade steel is level. If necessary, the blade surfaces are ground flat, e.g. by gluing sandpaper onto a level base and moving the blank across. Exact evenness is important for drilling the blade pivot at the precise angle. Then the outlines of the blade are transferred onto the steel. For this we use a scriber.

At the spot marking the blade pivot we center punch, drill, then ream the drill hole up to the size of the blade pivot, in our case 3.0 mm (0.118").

Transfer the outline of the blade from the template to the steel.

Center punch the position of the blade pivot so the drill bit doesn't wander.

At the center-punched position, drill with a diameter of 2.8 mm (0.110").

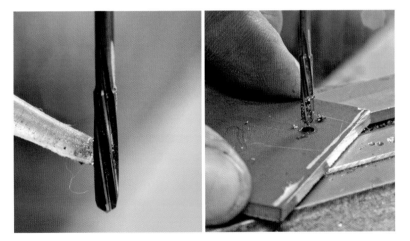

Then ream up to 3.0 mm (0.118"), making sure the bit is sufficiently lubricated.

Defining the blade shape is next. We drill a series of holes along the marked lines. With a coping saw or scroll saw, we then cut through the holes. Then we refine the shape with a coarse file. We continue with a smoother file. Leave some excess material at the base of the tang so we can work on the contact area with the spring later.

Drill just outside the scribed lines along the contour of the blade.

Cut through the holes with a coping saw or a scroll saw.

Clamp the blank in a vise. With a coarse file (cut 1 or cut 2) smooth out the surface.

During this step, we also check to make sure the blade fits inside the frame. If the blade tip sticks out a bit—as depicted in the photo—or there is not enough space for the spring, we correct this as necessary.

Check to make sure the blade fits into the frame. Correct any protruding parts. Leave some material at the tang, for adjusting the backspring later on.

The tang sticks out just a bit—mark the area to be filed off later.

The blade tip also sticks out a bit. You can adjust this later.

In order to file the pocket for the backspring, clamp the blade in the vise. First file the bottom of the pocket. The vice jaws act as a back stop and ensures that we achieve a level area on which the spring will later rest.

We start with the file and then continue with abrasive cloth up to P240. In order to work on the front edge of the pocket, we reposition the blade then file and sand as before. The length of our pocket is transferred from the template to the blade.

Once the blade is adjusted, clamp it in the vise. Use the hardened jaws of the vise as a back stop for the depth of the spring pocket.

File up to the level of the vice. In doing so, be sure not to file off or round the front end of the pocket.

Finish the filed corners with sand paper (P240).

To mark protruding areas, we place the blade onto one of the liners. An alignment pin serves as an auxiliary blade pivot. In our example, the shape of the blade's back doesn't fit with the handle. The blade is also protruding a bit around the guard. We mark these areas with a felt pen.

On the backside we transfer the shape of the spring from pocket to handle and check the position of the stop pin. We mark the area where the blade will hit.

Here the blade contour has been filed and the pocket shaped.

With help from the template, mark the rear edge of the pocket.

Connect the liner and blade with an alignment pin and mark the protruding areas of the blade.

With the blade fixed in open position, transfer the shape of the pocket onto the liner.

The hammer of the backspring reaches almost as far as the stop pin, but the hammer should not be close enough to rest on the stop pin when the blade is open.

With a hacksaw we first cut off the rear, protruding part of the tang. Afterwards, the blade will be assembled again and moved into the position it ought to have inside the closed knife. We mark the area where the spring will later rest on the tang. At the moment these marks are not identical to the final size—we leave a bit of material while working on this. The final adjustments of the tang and the spring will be done later on.

Roughly cut the blade tang to the correct size.

Transfer the spring position onto the closed blade.

Draw the positions of the stop pin and the front end of the liners.

With file and abrasive cloth we take the blade—clamped in the vise once again—down to the marked size. Then we prepare for grinding the blade. With the blade open, we mark the front outlines of the handle. A bit farther to the front we already marked the end stop of the blade, which should not extend to the edge—for this we mark the position through the drill hole in the liner with the blade closed.

With the waterproof pen and the blade clamped in the vise, we mark shoulder on both sides. This is the perimeter of the grinding. We don't scribe it—if we use the pen, we are always in control of our work, and later we won't have to remove deep grooves made by the scriber.

To determine the edge, we adjust a marking tool, a caliper gauge with scriber, or caliper to half the thickness of the edge from both sides. This way you can immediately see whether you hit the center or not. Later on we work exactly in symmetry on both sides of the blade. In order to see the line of the marking tool more clearly, it is helpful to grind the edge perpendicular to that line beforehand. As an alternative, layout dye can be used.

Parallel to the front end of the handle, mark the shoulder on both sides.

Scribe the edge of the blade with a caliper.

Now that the edge has been scribed, you can start grinding the blade.

For grinding the blade we use files and abrasive cloth. At the edge we leave between 0.2 mm (0.007") and 0.5 mm (0.019"). Final sharpening of the blade edge is only done after hardening.

To make things easier, we mount the blade to a lug that we can clamp in the vise. With the file, we then form the contours by grinding. While doing so, it is important to guide the file—and later the abrasive cloth—on top of the blade with the entire surface and not to tilt. Thus we get a consistent and even surface. We file cautiously and without applying too much pressure, otherwise the lug will come undone from the vice. Filing is done crosswise to achieve a clean, uniform surface.

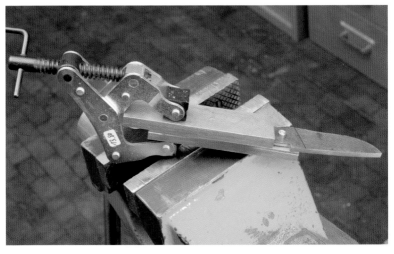

For grinding we use a lug. The blade is screwed in and the piece of metal on top prevents lateral movement.

We start with a coarse file, leaving a small area next to the shoulder unfiled. During the next step we use a finer mill saw file with rounded sides and work on the entire blade. With the mill saw file we achieve a clean curve at the shoulder.

With a coarse file, shape the blade from the edge.

Be careful to work on the whole area while retaining the transition towards the shoulder.

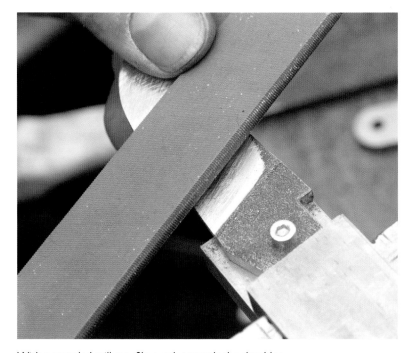

With a rounded mill saw file, work towards the shoulder.

With a rounded sanding block we work over the whole area again. While doing so, we take care to achieve a clean transition at the shoulder. We use abrasive cloth with grits P120, P240, and then P400. With each change of grits we change the direction of sanding as well—grit after grit is ground at an angle of 90° to the previous one. Here we should not change to a finer grit unless the whole surface is uniform and without scores or grooves. Besides that, we take care to achieve clear corners and not round the area at the shoulder or towards the back of the blade.

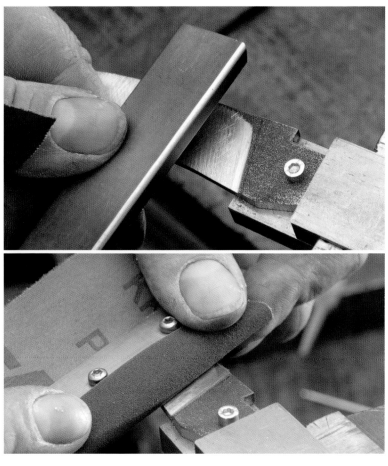

For work at the shoulder, use a proper sanding block.

# SPRING POCKET AND STOP PIN

With many traditional slipjoint folders, the blade can be pressed beyond the closed position towards and into the spring. This is bad for the blade and the backspring. A proper end stop keeps the blade away from the handle back. Either the end stop is constructed by means of an aptly shaped tang and backspring, or an additional stop pin is used.

about 2mm

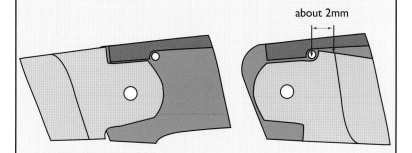

With respect to the position of the stop pin, you have to find a compromise. In our case the pin is located 2 mm (0.078") behind the blade edge.

We decide to use such a stop pin because it is easier to construct and manufacture. The stop pin is placed in such a way that it is located behind the edge for the closed blade and is hit by the tang.

The farther away from the main pivot the pin is located, the farther the end stop reaches into the area of the edge. The closer the pin is moved towards the pivot, the less space is left for the backspring—contact area and tang have to be shorter. The leverage of the spring holding the blade in place is also less

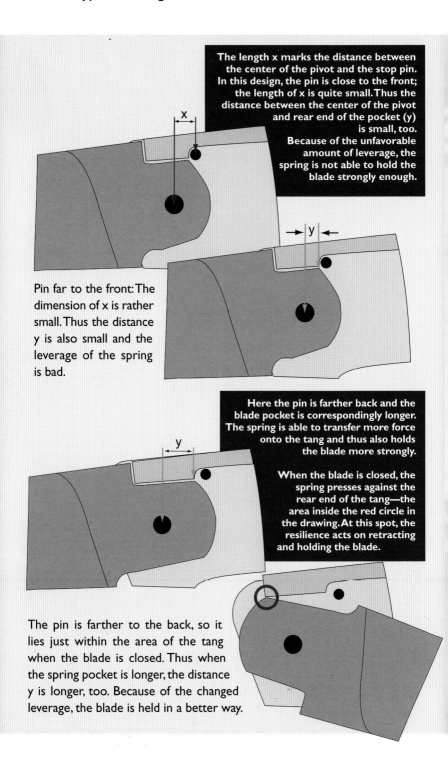

The length x marks the distance between the center of the pivot and the stop pin. In this design, the pin is close to the front; the length of x is quite small. Thus the distance between the center of the pivot and rear end of the pocket (y) is small, too. Because of the unfavorable amount of leverage, the spring is not able to hold the blade strongly enough.

Pin far to the front: The dimension of x is rather small. Thus the distance y is also small and the leverage of the spring is bad.

Here the pin is farther back and the blade pocket is correspondingly longer. The spring is able to transfer more force onto the tang and thus also holds the blade more strongly.

When the blade is closed, the spring presses against the rear end of the tang—the area inside the red circle in the drawing. At this spot, the resilience acts on retracting and holding the blade.

The pin is farther to the back, so it lies just within the area of the tang when the blade is closed. Thus when the spring pocket is longer, the distance y is longer, too. Because of the changed leverage, the blade is held in a better way.

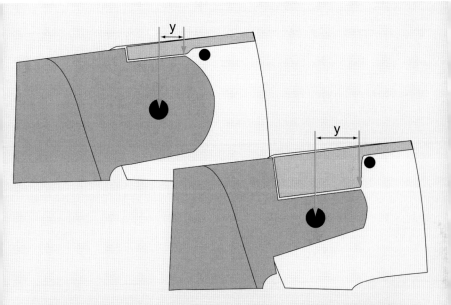

The larger the area of the tang around the pivot, the more space is left for big washers—the larger the surface area of the washer, the more stable the knife's action. The deeper the pocket for the spring, the smaller this area becomes.

On the other hand, with a deep pocket the corner on which the spring acts also moves backwards (the length of y). The leverage of the spring is better and the blade is held with more force.

The drafts are blown up a bit to better show how these parts interact. The ideal depth of the pocket is between the depicted extremes.

The deeper the pocket, the smaller the tang, i.e. the area which leads the blade inside the knife. The smaller this area, the more difficult it becomes to build an accurately moving and durable blade bearing. On the other hand, by increasing the depth of the pocket, the length of y also increases and the blade is held more strongly by the spring.

The construction of the stop pin and the pocket develops based on the end position, depth of the pocket, and height of the blade. Hence it is advisable to build a mockup out of cardboard, or better yet, brass, to test the function prior to building the actual knife.

## 2.4 Construction of the Backspring

Put a liner onto the raw material and roughly sketch the outlines. For spring steel we use 1.4112. As an alternative, any steel can be used that can be annealed to spring hardness. The spring—which is also used as a backspacer—should be as thick as the blade. Cutting the blade and spring from the same piece of raw material only requires you to grind the material down to the right thickness once.

With our knife we used washers for the blade, so the frame stands apart a bit at the front end. This in turn creates room for the spring to work freely. For a construction without washers, after hardening, the spring should be ground a bit, so it doesn't touch the liners and rub along them.

First, we work out the area which rests on the blade pocket. The contour of the blade pocket is transferred onto the spring blank. Using the liners that we have already drilled, we mark the position of the stop pin as a check. The spring must not go farther than this position.

Scribe the upper outline of the backspring along the liners.

With a hacksaw we roughly shape the profile of the hammer at the end of the spring. With files and abrasive cloth we start the precision work. In order to work at a right angle, we clamp the spring into the vise and use the jaws as a back stop for the corners. Polish the surfaces with abrasive cloth up to grit P400. Between each step, regularly check the fit of the spring inside the pocket.

Draw the shape of the hammer on the material.

Also mark the stop pin. The end of the backspring should not reach beyond the pin.

With the hacksaw, coarsely shape the contour of the hammer.

Use a file to refine the shape—the vise jaws work as a back stop.

Polish the area with a sanding block and sand paper (P400).

Check the fit of the spring and the length of the hammer.

File the front edge of the hammer at a right angle to the correct length and finish.

Remove burrs from the corners of the hammer.

After finishing the shape of the hammer, line up the spring and blade and fix the spring, blade, and liners with clamps. Now, using the previously drilled liner, we mark the position of the drill holes through which our blade will later be riveted. As we did with the liners, first drill, then ream the holes up to the desired size.

Fix the blade in open position.

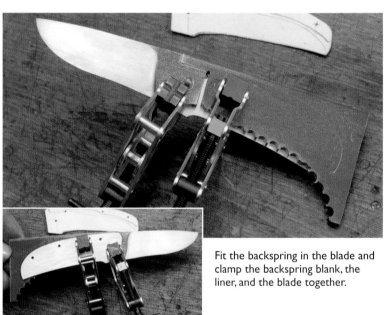

Fit the backspring in the blade and clamp the backspring blank, the liner, and the blade together.

Using the holes in the liner, drill the holes through the spring.

While reaming the drill holes, be sure to lubricate the bit.

We fasten the spring to the liner (with alignment pins, if required) and again scribe the outline. We do the coarse work with a hacksaw. Similar to the work on the blade, we then refine the shape with files and abrasive cloth (up to P240).

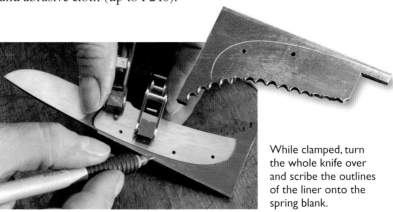

While clamped, turn the whole knife over and scribe the outlines of the liner onto the spring blank.

With a hacksaw, roughly saw along the scribed line.

Shape the outer contour of the spring with file and sandpaper.

To work flush with the liners, the spring, blade, and liners are assembled again with the alignment pins and clamped in the vise. In order to outline the inner contours, we first scribe the front, springy part of the backspring. The shape of the rear part is determined by the position of the blade inside the closed knife. We now draw the outline, while leaving enough room for the blade.

Mount the blade, spring blank, and liners with alignment pins.

In the vise, finish the outer contour of the spring.

With a caliper, scribe the inner contour of the spring parallel to the top edge.

The rear part of the spring mirrors the shape of the blade.

Just in front of the front drill hole, the thicker, rear area narrows down to become the thin, springy front part. We draw this transition as a soft curve. In the front, between the hammer and the stationary part of the spring, the thickness of the spring measures a constant 2.0 mm (0.078"). Again, we drill along the line and cut through the holes with a coping saw or scroll saw. After that, we continue as usual: filing and grinding up to P400.

Draw the transition to the springy part.

Drill along the marked outline.

With a coping saw or scroll saw, cut through the excess material between the drill holes.

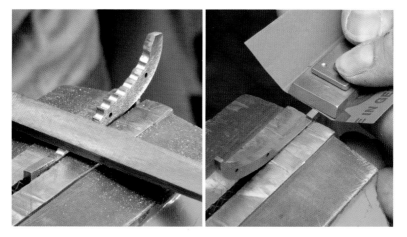

Refine the outline with files and sandpaper.

It is important to form a clean transition between the springy part and the stationary part of the backspring. Thus you avoid notch brittleness and fatigue fractures. To do so, we use proper semicircular files and rounded sanding blocks.

Don't test the performance of the backspring at this point! Unhardened, the spring would be permanently bent.

## 2.5 Finishing the Tang

Mount the blade to the liner with an alignment pin. In closed position, through the drill hole in the liner, we mark the position where our stop pin rests. Clamp the blade into the vise and shape the area with a file, round file, and sandpaper. While doing so, repeatedly check the required depth.

When the blade stop fits, remove material from the corners of the tang until the tang is able to move past the stop pin. As an aid, the area can be drawn on the blade through the drill hole of the stop pin by means of a pen.

Mark the position of the stop pin through the hole in the liner.

Shape the recess for the stop pin with a round file.

Regularly check the depth of the recess.

The tang hits the stop pin. The excess material in this area has to be removed.

Through the stop pin hole in the liner, mark the excess on the tang.

With file and sandpaper, the corners are accordingly removed and the tang is ground circular. During opening and closing, the backspring glides on this surface. The curve should thus be uniform and polished cleanly.

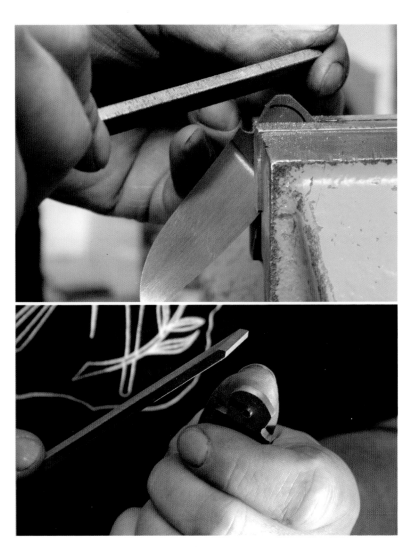

With file and sandpaper, shape the radius.

During the next work step we shape the area of the tang, which is hit by the spring in closed position. Spring and handle back ought to be flush in this position as well. For this we remove material from the tang. Blade and spring are placed on the liner; the blade is closed up to the end stop. We lift the spring slightly and let it rest on the blade. The excess is marked on the tang.

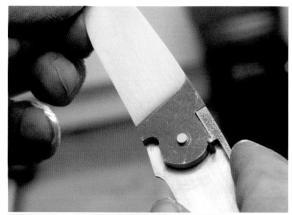

Quality Control: The hammer protrudes above the liners with the blade in closed position. We have to refine the tang so the hammer sits flush.

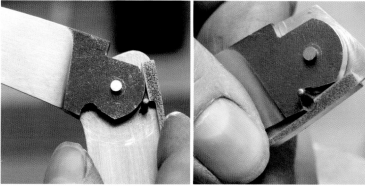

This part of the tang has to be ground off.

Using a slight bevel, file the area between the recess for the stop pin and the rear part of the tang, onto which the spring presses in closed position. The spring ought to act on the rear edge and thus pull the blade into the handle. Towards the stop pin, there ought to be a bit of space.

As in the previous steps, we file and grind this area up to P400. In between, we repeatedly check the progress of our work, so the spring won't be located too deep later on.

Gradually we work towards achieving the right shape; the spring has to be flush with the liners in open and closed position. Finally, we again polish all the surfaces. For a clean finish around the blade pivot, we polish with P400 on a plane surface.

Regularly check the position of the spring.

The excess of the spring is clear—this amount has to be taken off the tang.

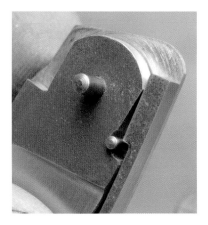

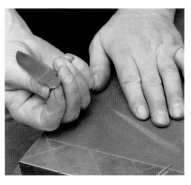

On a flat surface, polish the lateral surfaces of the tang.

The spring is now flush with the liner.

Here the surfaces have been finished to grit P400.

## 2.6 Precision Work on the Blade and Spring

Polish the lateral surfaces and the back of the blade with grit P600. For the final polish of the blade we only work in one direction—from the blade foot to the tip. While doing so, we take care to keep well-defined edges at the shoulder and towards the back.

The spring is also polished all around up to P600. To achieve the required initial tension, we cautiously bend the spring downwards about 2 mm (0.078").

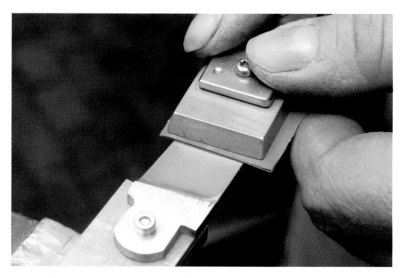

Finish with P600 lengthwise on a hard and level surface.

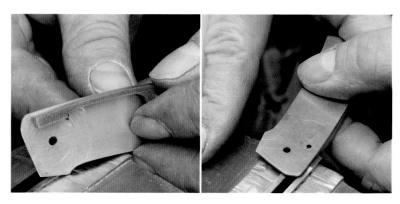

Clamp the spring in a vise with smooth jaws and pre-bend it slightly.

Now the blade and spring can be hardened and heat-treated. The blade is hardened to a case hardness of about 58 to 61 HRC, depending on the steel type; the spring is hardened to around 45 HRC.

For the spring to move smoothly along the blade, we also polish the inside up to P800.

The blade and spring are back from being hardened/annealed.

Prior to further work, cautiously polish the spring again to P800.

## 2.7. Intermediate Check and Washers

After hardening, mount the spring inside the handle and check the initial tension. If necessary, we can cautiously bend it a bit further. For the spring to move smoothly along the blade, we polish the inside up to P800. Thereafter the spring is once again placed inside the handle.

With a hollow punch, we stamp two washers out of teflon with a thickness of 0.1 mm (0.003"). The outer diameter measures 12 mm (0.472") and fits the space on the blade tang; the inner diameter matches the pivot, which is 3.0 mm (0.118").

With the help of alignment pins, we assemble blade, spring, and stop pin. In case the blade does not move easily around the pivot after heat treatment, we cautiously widen the drill hole with a diamond cutter (Dremel, Proxxon, etc.) or a round diamond needle file.

Assemble the spring with alignment pins for testing. The initial tension value is 2 mm (0.078").

With two hollow punches, punch the washers out of teflon foil.

Assemble the knife to test it.

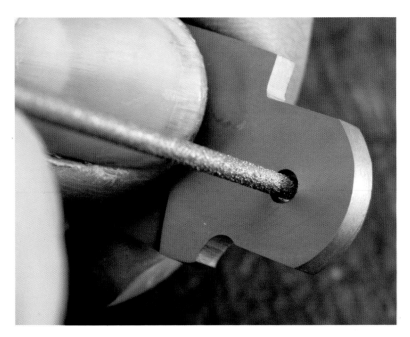

If the blade pivot is too tight, cautiously widen the drill hole with a diamond file.

Prior to the next steps we check the performance of our knife. Is the end stop alright in open and closed position? Is the tension of the spring sufficient? Are all the parts flush? If necessary, we touch up necessary areas.

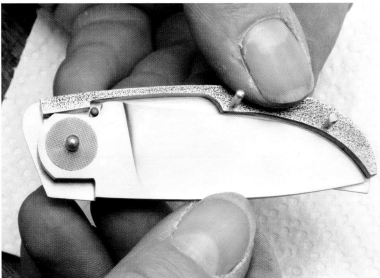

The test lets you know if you've followed the process correctly so far.

Now the blade is polished, once again, evenly along its length with P600, then P800.

The part of the tang the spring hammer moves along is also polished as much as possible or even buffed. The smoother the surface, the softer the blade movement will be when opening and closing the knife.

Finish the tang on a flat surface with P800.   Give the surfaces of the blade a final polish up to P800.

The blade looks great after the final polish.

## 2.8 Handle Scales

First of all, we make sure that the handle material is large and flat enough to lay flat and cover the entire surface of the liners. If necessary, grind the handle material flat with sandpaper.

Then glue the liners to the handle material, in this case yew.

Glue the liner to the handle scale with an epoxy glue.

After the glue has set, grind the excess glue off.

previously drilled to make the holes for attaching the spring as well as the blade pivot. Do not drill all the way through for the stop pin.

With a saw we coarsely outline the contours. With file and sandpaper up to P240 we work step by step towards the final shape of the handle scales. File and polish the profile to a rounded shape. Afterwards, the corners at the inside of the liners are slightly rounded/trimmed.

Pivot and rivets are prepared. For this we use bronze rods of the proper

Drill the holes for the rivets through the liners. For the stop pin, we drill approximately 2 mm (0.078") deep, which gives us more tolerance when cutting the pin to size.

With a table saw, roughly cut the contours of the handle scale.

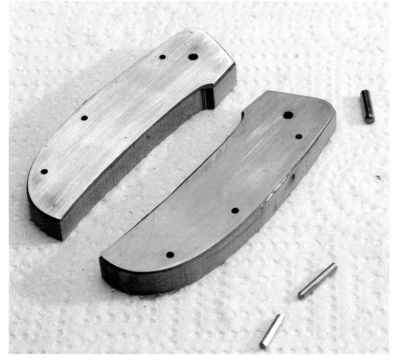

Then finish the shape with a file and sandpaper.

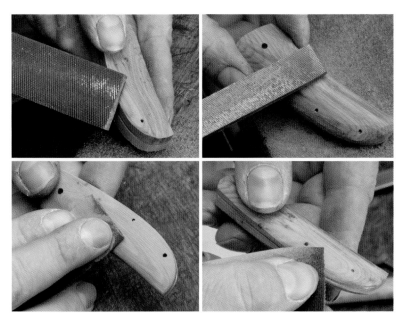

File and sand the three-dimensional contours of the handle.

Slightly round the inner contours of the liners.

diameter and cut them into adequate pieces. To determine the right length, measure while holding the parts of the knife together and add 1.0 mm (0.039") to 1.5 mm (0.059") in order to have enough material for riveting. The ends of the rods are deburred prior to assembly.

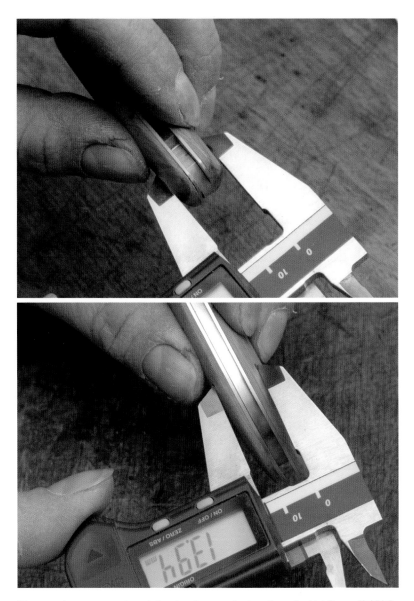

Measure the necessary length for the rivets at the handle and add 1.5 mm (0.059").

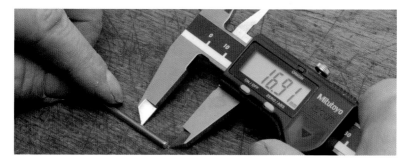

Scribe the length of the rivet on an appropriate round material.

Cut the rivets to size with a saw and remove the burrs with a file.

Everything is ready for the final assembly.

## 2.9 Assembly and Finish

We put the parts of our knife together and once again check the performance prior to riveting.

Assemble the parts of the knife.

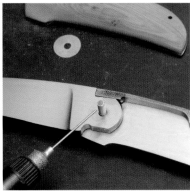

A drop of oil about to fall, the blade moves smoothly once and for all.

Prior to riveting, the knife is completely assembled.

While riveting with the hammer, you should not hit too hard, otherwise the wood around the rivet may crack. The rivet can be pressed in the vise a bit first. Then the rivets are clenched with the hammer on an appropriate surface. In between we check the movements of the blade and the specifications of the handle.

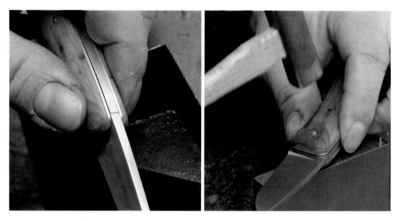

With careful blows of the hammer, flatten the ends of the rivet like a mushroom.

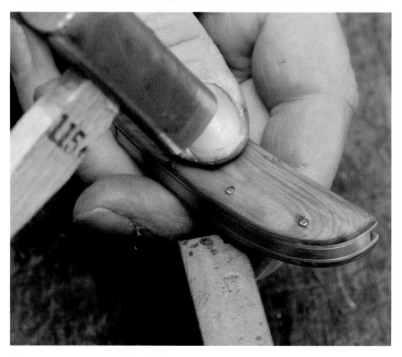

Check the movement of the blade several times in between flattening the rivets.

After we have finished riveting the knife, we cautiously rework the rivet heads in order to match them with the handle contours. The final finish is done by means of smooth sandpaper.

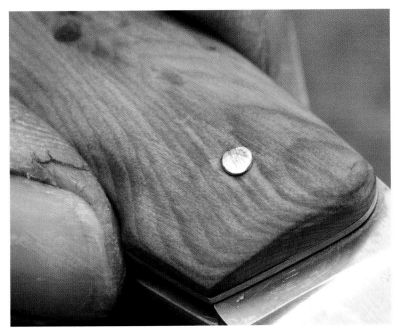

Remove the excess material from the rivet so it is flush with the handle.

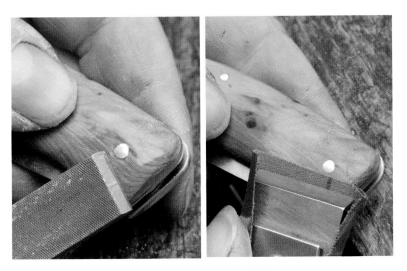

Finish the surface with a file and sandpaper (up to P600).

To protect the wood, we rub linseed oil or hard wax onto the handle scales. We sharpen the blade edge with a diamond file. Our slipjoint folder is now completely finished!

Rub linseed oil into the wood using a piece of cloth.

Finally, sharpen the edge of the blade with a diamond stone.

Simple and beautiful: the finished slipjoint folder.

## 2.10 Variations

## 2.10.1 Blade Tang

With this variation, the blade tang is not shaped as a radius. During opening/closing, the spring hammer lies flat on the rear of the tang. This acts as a "resting stop" halfway along the way.

Remark: With this knife, you can clearly see what can go wrong. The stop pin was placed a bit too close to the front. Thus the corners of the tang had to be rounded for the tang to pass by. By rounding the corners, a few millimeters of the area onto which the spring could have acted were given away. In closed position (opposite below) it is obvious that there would have been enough space to move the stop pin farther to the back.

Knife halfway opened: here the spring rests on the tang noticeably.

Optimization: Notice the position of the stop pin, the stop area, the end of the edge, and the position of the hammer.

## 2.10.2 Pivot Variations

If you would like to have the possibility to exchange the blade or to adjust its play, a variation with a pivot that is screwed together is obviously the best choice. An easy solution is to buy brass pivot pins and fitting head screws at a home improvement store.

To shorten the pivot, we use a piece of material that fits the desired length—in this case a piece of aluminum. We drill a hole of the same diameter as the pivot and use our auxiliary piece as a back stop while filing. This way we can be sure that the pivot is shortened at a right angle.

Use pivot pins from a home improvement store for the screw connections of the axis.

The pivot pin in the auxiliary piece.

The finished pivot and a fitting screw.

Interesting variation: Slipjoint folder with a screwed-in blade pivot.

A scaly design: screwed-in blade pivot, liners of nickel silver, and glued and riveted ziricote wood handle scales.

Another version: Soldered bronze bolsters, brass liners, and handle scales of kudu horn.

# Friction Folding Knife

The "friction" in the term "friction folder" refers to the friction between the blade and handle of this type of knife. Friction is the only force holding the blade in the open and closed position.

At the front end of the handle, we bend a ferrule around the wood. Later, the blade pivot will be guided and riveted with this ferrule. At the same time, the ferrule acts as an end stop for the blade.

We forego an end stop in closed position because the blade of our knife doesn't rest on metal but on the wood of the handle.

## 3.1 Designing and Drawing a Template

As with the slipjoint project, first draw the design on graph paper. A guideline marks the center of our knife, a second one depicts the desired blade length. First we draw the blade tang and plot the position of the blade pivot—again, a bit below the center. Now we design the blade shape up to the first guideline.

Three guidelines mark the center, the blade length, and the height of our knife.

Then we place the point of a compass on the pivot and transfer the blade length backwards—the handle must be at least this long in order to cover the blade completely in closed position. Draw the handle; its width depends on the dimensions of the blade. Towards the end of the handle, slope the handle downwards a bit. This way there is a bit more room for the tip of the blade and the knife will sit more securely in our hand.

Within the boundaries of the guidelines, draw the blade shape.

With a compass, transfer the blade length and thus determine the back edge of the handle.

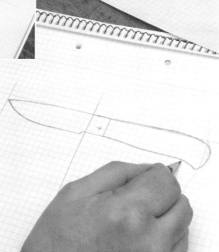

Draw the desired handle shape—the handle gets broader towards the end and extends slightly beyond the radius to securely cover the blade tip.

We transfer the drawing onto cardboard and cut out the contours; leave some excess material around the tang. A thumbtack serves as the pivot so we can check that the blade and handle fit together. If necessary, we can refine the contours.

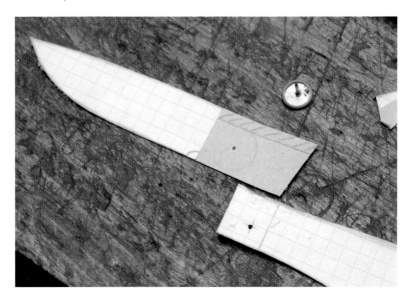

Cut out the template transferred onto cardboard and assemble. Cut off any protruding parts, e.g. excess material at the tang.

We close the blade far enough for the tip to be covered by the handle. Draw the outline of the blade inside the handle. The handle must be cut this far later on.

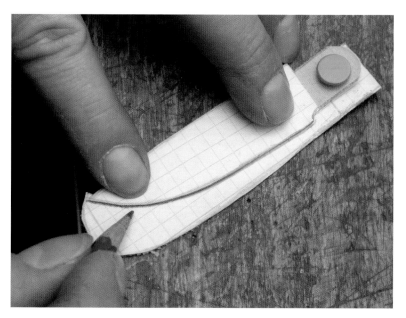

Determine the closed position of the blade and transfer the outline of the edge onto the handle.

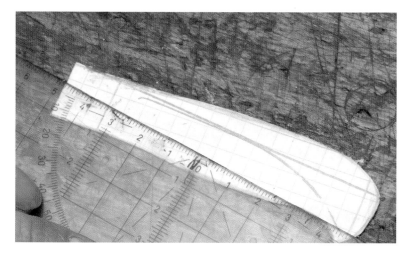

The straight line depicts how deeply we'll have to saw into the handle later on.

## 3.2 Creating the Blade

Transfer the shape of the blade onto the blade material. For the friction folder we use N690 flat steel with a thickness of 1.5 mm (0.059").

With a hacksaw we roughly saw the steel. Along the marked contours of the blade we drill holes, then cut through the remaining material with a coping saw or scroll saw. With file and sandpaper —just like the process for the slipjoint folder—we finish the contours. Leave some excess material at the tang; final adjustments will be done later.

Transfer the outline of the blade onto the steel.

With a hacksaw, roughly saw the contour of the blade.

Drill holes along the scribed outline and cut through the holes with a coping saw or scroll saw.

As with the slipjoint folder, file the contour of the blade.

## 3.3 Working on the Handle

The ferrule on the handle holds the rivet that will act as the blade pivot. We use a piece of spring steel for this. Also suitable, and perhaps easier to work with, would be a pin of brass or bronze. With a caliper, we scribe the desired width—layout dye enhances the visibility of the scribed lines.

Use the dimensions of the other parts of the knife to determine the ferrule's measurements. The width of the ferrule should be enough to cover the tang. The length of the metal strip is the circumference of the handle (diameter times 3.14 for a spherical profile) plus a few extra millimeters—the corners often can't be bent completely and look ugly after hammering. This area is cut off later on.

Saw the ferrule out and clamp it in a vice to remove burrs with a file. Here we also use the clamping jaws as a back stop to make sure that the corners remain parallel.

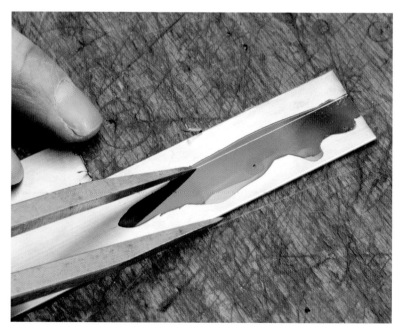

Scribe the width of the ferrule.

Coarsely saw the ferrule out, then finish in the vise. The clamping jaws act as a back stop and helps create a flat surface.

Bend the ferrule around a pipe. Depending on the handle shape, this could have a round or oval shape. Round the ferrule out evenly with a hammer. Saw off the part that is too long. Using the vise, bend the ends close together. In doing this, regularly check that the ferrule is keeping its round shape. Finally, we take the burrs off the edge of the ferrule.

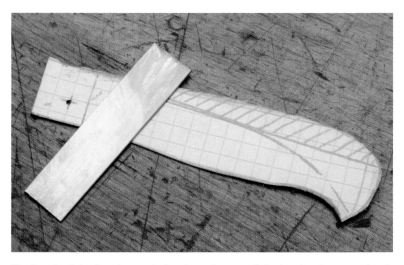

The length of the ferrule equals the circumference of the handle plus a couple of additional millimeters.

Bend the ferrule around a piece of appropriate round material.

If the ends of the ferrule overlap, cut them off. Finish bending the ferrule with the vise. Check the ferrule often in order to achieve a clean curvature.

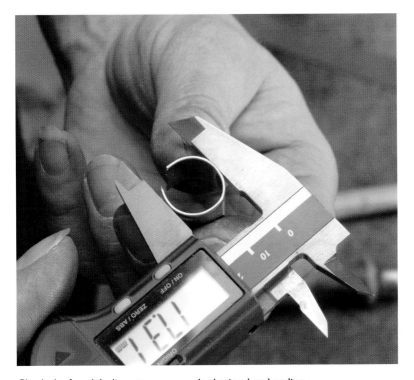

Check the ferrule's diameter on a regular basis when bending.

Place the ferrule in the vice and remove burrs with a file.

Parts of the template, the raw blade, and ferrule.

On the wood piece for the handle, mark the area where the ferrule will later wrap around the handle. With a wood saw, roughly cut out the front part of the handle.

On the handle wood, mark the area where the ferrule will wrap around the handle.

Saw out the area where the ferrule will be placed.

On the front part of the handle, outline the ferrule's shape. Cut out the shape roughly with the saw, then round out the cylinder with a file and sandpaper until the ferrule fits tightly on the handle.

To create the cylinder shape for the handle, use the ferrule as a template.

Work on the surface of the cylinder with file and sandpaper until the ferrule fits tightly.

Now we draw the complete handle shape on the wooden handle. Mark the area where the blade rests in closed position—we have to saw this far into the handle from the bottom. After that, mark the center of the handle on the bottom of the wood. As an indication for sawing, mark the centerline and its depth on the rear end of the handle.

Transfer the handle shape onto the wood.

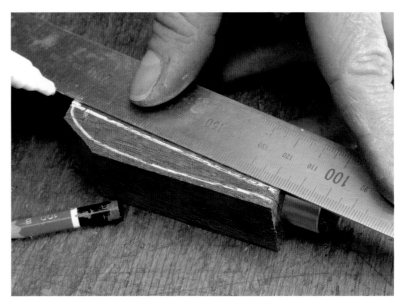

Measure the depth of the required cut on the template and transfer it to the handle.

Mark the center of the handle. Clamp the wood in a vise along the drawn depth of the cut. For orientation during sawing, we also draw the center line and depth of the cut on the end of the wood.

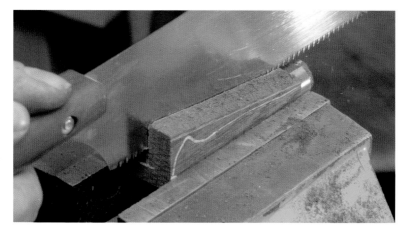

Cut the handle along the marked lines.

With a saw we cut the groove into the handle along the centerline and to the marked depth. The groove has to be widened just far enough for the blade to slip into the handle—if the blade has too much play, there won't be enough friction for the handle to hold the blade in.

Use the blade to check whether the handle groove is wide enough. If necessary, refine the slot with a broader saw blade. If the saw blades are too thin, you can use spacers and saw along them.

Starting coarsely and then progressively using smoother files, we shape the profile of the handle step by step. With sandpaper, give the handle its final shape (for round handles, abrasive cloth is helpful).

With files and sandpaper, create the handle's shape.

## 3.4 Grinding the Blade

With the blade clamped in the vise, we mark the shoulder on both sides. Scribe the blade's edge from both sides.

For filing, clamp the blade tightly in the vise. Again, we file crosswise up to about 0.1 mm (0.003") to the scribed edge. The procedure is identical to that of the slipjoint folder. Finish with sandpaper up to P400. A hard sanding block is helpful in achieving a clean corner at the shoulder.

With the blade adjusted and clamped in the vise, mark the shoulder on both sides.

Scribe the center of the blade from both sides with a caliper.

Fix the blade on top of the vise with two clamps.

File the lateral surface of the blade.

With the blade clamped on the vise, file the blade tip. Use light pressure to prevent the blade from moving sideways.

Towards the shoulder, use a mill saw file. This allows you to create the transition to a clean corner at the shoulder.

Remove file marks with sandpaper and a sanding block. Start with grit P180, then work from P240 to P400.

## 3.5 Connecting the Ferrule with Blade and Handle

We mount the ferrule onto the handle. Check the width and depth of the groove again and fine tune if necessary.

Push the blade into the handle until it stops at the ferrule and adjust it in open position. The pivot is placed a bit below the center. With a caliper we take the measurement from our template and mark the height of the pivot on both sides of the ferrule. Perpendicular to that we scribe the center of the drill hole on both sides.

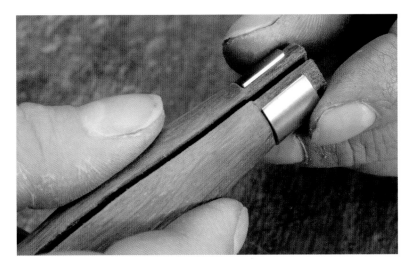

Mount the ferrule on the handle.

Push the blade into the handle and check that it fits in the groove tightly.

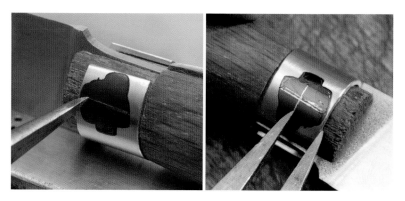

Scribe the height of the pivot on both sides. For this we use layout dye, caliper, and an auxiliary base as a back stop for the caliper. Now we determine the center of the drill hole for the blade pivot.

We center punch so the drill bit doesn't wander.

Since we have to drill on a round surface, we center punch the ferrule at the pivot so the drill bit doesn't wander. Cautiously we drill at the marked position through ferrule, handle, and blade. For this, we pre-drill on each side with the knife resting on an angle. Then place the knife blade flat on the vise and drill all the way through the knife.

Pre-drill through the sheet metal into the wood on one side with the knife turned at a slight angle.

Repeat on the opposite side of the knife.

Now drill through the entire knife with the blade lying flat on top of the vise.

After drilling we take our knife apart and remove burrs and other irregularities with sandpaper. The blade tang should be round to prevent corners from protruding from the handle. With a curve template, we draw the desired contour around the drill hole of the pivot. Shape the tang with file and sandpaper.

Draw the curvature of the tang with a curve template.

Using the vise, file the shape of the tang.

In order to check whether the tang fits into the handle, we temporarily assemble the blade on the outside. The blade has to sit within the handle deep enough during opening and closing the knife. If not, we have to refine.

Mount the blade on the outside and check that there is enough room for the tang inside the handle.

Assemble the knife, using a drill bit as the blade pivot, to check the knife in closed position.

The knife can't be closed completely. Thus we deepen the groove in the handle a bit more.

For this preliminary quality control test, an appropriately sized drill bit acts as the blade pivot. With our knife, the blade tip isn't covered by the handle when in closed position. The groove is not deep enough—with a saw, we refine step by step until the blade is able to dip deep enough into the handle.

The part of the handle that protrudes above the ferrule is also filed and sanded so the handle is flush with the ferrule. With sandpaper we clean the corners of the groove. At this point the handle wood can be sealed. For this we use Danish Oil, which we rub into the handle with a piece of cloth. Be cautious with products made from linseed oil: moist pieces of cloth can ignite spontaneously after a while!

File off the protruding part of the wood and sand.

Round the inside corners of the groove slightly.    Treat the handle with linseed oil.

The parts of the friction folder prior to hardening the blade.

## 3.6 Assembly and Finish

Before we sharpen the edge, we take the knife to the heat treatment company to be annealed. When informed about the steel type, the person doing the heat treatment knows the required temperatures for hardening and annealing. In our case, the blades were hardened in a vacuum and annealed to 59 HRC.

Once hardened, we satin polish the surface of the blade up to grit P800. For this we also use the sanding block and only work in one direction—from the foot of the blade to the tip.

For the pivot we use a 3.0 mm (0.118") rod of stainless steel, which we cut to the desired length; for riveting, about 1 mm (0.039") should be left on each side. Prior to assembly, remove burrs from both sides.

After hardening, we strop the blade lengthwise with P800.

Determine the required length of the pivot.

Transfer the length onto the rod and add 2 mm (0.078").

Cut the pivot to size and remove burrs from the ends.

Push the pivot through. We, once again, check that the knife is functioning properly. If everything fits, the ferrule is riveted. For this we use a proper base (anvil, steel block) and cautiously hammer from both sides alternately. In between, regularly check the movement of the blade. Is the blade too tight? If you cautiously break the knife in by moving the blade to and fro a bit, it should start to move a bit more freely.

Insert the pivot and rivet it on a hard surface.

Use a hammer and the vise for riveting. Be sure not to hit the ferrule during this process.

As a final step we sharpen the edge of the blade with a diamond file. The handle is finished with hard wax. The friction folder is now ready for work!

Finally, sharpen the edge with a diamond file.

Seal the handle with hard wax all around.

A timeless tool: the finished friction folder.